PELÉ

by Bill Gutman

GROSSET & DUNLAP
A Filmways Company
PUBLISHERS ● NEW YORK

Picture Credits: Joe Di Maggio, cover; Joe Bereswill, pages 10, 15, 22, 50, 55, 62, 67, 69, 70, 74–75, 78–79, 84–85, 90; Wide World, ii, vi, 25, 29, 32, 36, 39, 43, 45, 49, 52, 59, 66, 89, 92, 95.

CONTENTS

CHAPTER 1

His real name is Edson Arantes do Nascimento. But millions of sports fans from South America, to Europe, to Africa, to the Middle East, to Russia, simply call him Pelé. He is easily the best known athlete in the whole world.

It might be hard to believe that this man called Pelé is better known than Henry Aaron, O.J. Simpson, Julius Erving, or Bobby Orr. For Pelé doesn't play baseball, football, basketball, or hockey. He plays another sport. His sport is the most popular sport in almost every country in the world, except America.

His sport is soccer. The man they call Pelé is known as the King of Soccer. He has held that title for some 20 years. In fact, most people agree that he is the greatest soccer player ever.

It's difficult for an American to really understand Pelé's greatness. For in this country soccer is still a young and growing sport. But look at it this way. Pick one of the four major sports in America—baseball, football, basketball, hockey—and ask fans to name its greatest player. Then watch the arguments start.

Cobb / Ruth / DiMaggio / Aaron; Brown / Simpson, Unitas / Namath / Jurgensen; Chamberlain / Russell / Abdul-Jabbar, Robertson / West, Baylor / Erving; Richard / Howe / Hull / Orr / Clarke. Those are just some of the names that come up when people try to decide who's the best player of one of these popular sports.

Not so with soccer fans. No matter what language they speak, what team they root for, what country they're from, they all say the same thing when asked about the greatest.

Pelé.

He is the one and only. There is no argument. There never was. Not since the time the 15-year-old Pelé first played for the Santos team in his native Brazil. All he did after just two years of playing with them was lead Santos to the World Cup Championship. In fact, Pelé played for Santos of Brazil in four World Cup tournaments. And Santos won three of them!

The World Cup is like the World Series, only bigger. It's held once every four years and is open to teams the world over. So the team that wins the World Cup is truly the World Champion. There are sometimes 400 million people from all countries

watching the World Cup on television. That's how important soccer is around the world. And that's how many people have seen Pelé play. All those people know he is the greatest.

At the end of the 1974 season, Pelé said he was retiring. He was nearly 34 years old and had been playing a long time. He did retire—but not for long. In 1975, Pelé came to America to play soccer for the New York Cosmos.

The Cosmos play in the North American Soccer League. It's a new league, having just started in 1967. But it's a very important league because, for the first time, soccer has a chance to become a major sport in the United States. That's why the Cosmos wanted Pelé. And that's why Pelé wanted to play for the Cosmos.

"What I find strange," said Pelé, "is that New York, which is the world capitol of sports, ignores soccer, the

Pelé gets a hearty welcome as he walks onto the field to play his first game as a Cosmos.

most widely played sport in the world. Football and baseball are so widely accepted there that people have forgotten soccer, but I am sure I can help to revive it."

It seems like the perfect marriage, Though soccer isn't that popular in the United States, Pelé's name is still magic. More and more fans are coming out to see him, and many more youngsters are playing the game than ever before. Perhaps Pelé is right. Someday soccer will be as popular as baseball and football in the United States.

What about this game called soccer? How did it become so popular throughout the whole world? And why isn't it really popular in America? There are many questions to be answered since the game is quite different from baseball, football, basketball, and hockey.

Soccer is a fast game, with nonstop action. It is played on a field from 100 to 130 yards long, and 50 to 100 yards wide. Different fields have slightly different measurements. There are 11 players on each side. One is a goalkeeper, who must protect a goal that is 8 feet high and 24 feet wide.

He must protect it from the 10 other players who are trying to kick or head a leather ball past him.

The ball is slightly smaller than a basketball and slightly larger than a volleyball. Good soccer players can kick it at almost 80 miles an hour.

There are many different ways to kick the soccer ball. Most players use the instep, or inside part of their foot. They can control the ball better that way. Just look at all the soccer players who have become placekickers in the National Football League. Men like Pete Gogolak, Jan Stenerud, Garo

Yepremian, Roy Gerela, and Chester Marcol were all soccer players who still kick with their insteps.

The goalkeeper stops the ball any way he can—with his hands, body, or feet. He often leaps and dives to stop a shot. The other players, of course, cannot use their hands. They can only use their feet, head, or body to move the ball. But soccer players are magicians with their feet and can "dribble" the ball as well as a hockey player with a stick.

A soccer game consists of two, 45-minute periods, each of which is played with no time-outs. The action is fast and furious. But all 10 players don't swarm after the ball at once. There are positions other than the goalkeeper, much like hockey. In soccer there are attackmen, linkmen, and defensemen.

Many soccer teams use four de-

Pelé follows through after heading the ball at the goal.

fensemen. They are: two centerbacks, a right back and a left back. The right and left backs usually cover the attacking outside forwards. The center backs guard the middle of the field. That's where the attacking "strikers" usually play. The centerbacks must also be able to start the attack going. They are the quarterbacks of the defense and can really control the game.

In front of the four defenders are usually two linkmen. (They used to be called midfielders or halfbacks.) The linkmen connect the defense with the attacking forwards. They must swing from defense to attack—from attack back to defense. A linkman is constantly moving. It is a difficult position since he must have all the defensive as well as attacking skills. He must try to be where the ball is, or near enough to get into the action immediately.

The front line in soccer usually consists of four attackmen who cover two outside forwards and two inside forwards. The inside forwards are called "strikers." Although he can play anywhere on the field, Pelé usually plays a striker position with the Cosmos.

The strikers are generally the team's best goal scorers. Other players try to set them up. They must be able to shoot with power and accuracy with either foot. And they must also be good "headers." Since soccer players can't use their hands, they often use their heads to pass or shoot the ball.

Outside forwards must be very fast and good ball handlers. They must also be able to pass well and get the ball inside to the strikers. Good, fast outside forwards help keep the defense spread out, and can tire a defense by making them work extra hard. Soccer is a rougher game than many people think. Players can be hurt at any time.

There is a great deal of body contact. When a player tries to get the ball from another player the move is called "tackling." But it's not the same as in American football. One tackling move is the shoulder charge—impact between the shoulders of two players. Sometimes they hit very hard.

Another tackling move is with the feet. The defensive players lunge to get the ball. This move often results in a tangle of legs and some nasty falls. When several players leap at once to try to head the ball, hard body contact can often result.

There is a great deal of excitement in a soccer match. Fans the world over can't wait to see their favorite teams play. There were more than 200,000 fans in Maracana Stadium in Rio de Janeiro, Brazil, to see the 1950 World Cup final. Countries have sometimes even come to the brink of war over a hard-fought soccer game.

It's difficult to say exactly when the game of soccer started. There have always been ballgames, played with many different kinds of balls. But modern soccer is said to have been born in England sometime in the middle 1800s. There wasn't much order in the games. The players all rushed around after the ball. They were trying to put it between the goal, which was made of two wooden posts with another across the top.

In 1863, the first rules of soccer were written in London. Now, there are various rules and regulations in the sport. If you watch a few games, you can learn the rules quickly. The action is fast, but the scores are not usually high. They are much like hockey scores.

Soon after the establishment of those 1863 rules, the game began to spread around the world. It was spread by British seamen who visited almost every port on the globe. Whenever the ships docked, the seamen would go ashore and start a soccer game in order to relax. Local people watched them. Soon they copied the sailors.

Soccer was also spread by British businessmen who worked in the different countries. They would set up teams for their workers to keep them happy. Pretty soon the workers were playing on their own time and showing the game to their friends. By the early 1900s, the modern game of soccer had been spread around the world by the British. And by the 1920s, many countries were producing their own great teams and great players.

Soccer came to the United States in the 1800s in much the same way. Some colleges began playing almost immediately. Many people think Princeton and Rutgers played the first college football game in 1869. But the game they played that afternoon was closer to soccer than to American football.

Pretty soon most Americans were turning to a new game of their own. It was called baseball, and it also started in 1869 with the first professional team. Soccer remained at some colleges. But it was played mostly by people who had come to America from other countries. American football and the rough game of rugby both grew out of soccer. But soccer itself didn't really grow at all.

By the turn of the century, baseball was the number one sport in America. Football was very popular in the colleges, and basketball was also starting. In Canada, ice hockey was growing very rapidly. Soccer was only a minor sport played by a small number of people. It would remain that way in the United States until 1967. That's a pretty long time.

CHAPTER 2

But even before professional soccer really got its start in the United States, Edson Arantes do Nascimento was showing the rest of the world how the game of soccer should be played. The man known as Pelé played his first game for Santos in his native Brazil in 1956. He was just 15 years old then, a boy playing against men. But he quickly showed everyone that he was going to be great.

He was to remain a worldwide superstar for the next 18 years. In that time, Pelé scored 1,220 goals in about 1,250 games. That's nearly a goal-a-game average, which is an amazing feat for a soccer player. Here's what one writer said about Pelé:

"The goals he scores are often over-shadowed by the seemingly magical sequence that precedes them—his uncanny control, his sudden bursts of acceleration, his instinctive positioning, his inventive passes."

Pelé is a complete soccer player. He can do everything possible on the soccer field. And he does some things that seem impossible as well. How did Pelé become the world's greatest soccer player? As with so many great athletes, he was born with natural talents. Then he found in himself the desire and drive to develop those talents to the fullest.

Edson Arantes do Nascimento was born on October 23, 1940, in a Brazilian village called Tres Coracoes, which means "Three Hearts." He was the

Pelé posed at New York's Herald Square in 1966
when he was with Brazil's Santos team on a visit.

first child of Dondinho and Celeste Nascimento. His father was a professional soccer player also. But in those days soccer players did not make much money, and the family was quite poor.

In 1942, Edson's brother Zoca was born. And four years later a sister, Maria Luci, was the third child. In 1946, the family moved to the town of Bauru in San Paulo, Brazil. They moved so Dondinho Nascimento could play center forward (or striker) for the Bauru Atletico Clube.

Young Edson was already in love with the game of soccer. He watched his father very often and liked it when the older man would kick the ball around with him. He made his first soccer ball out of a tangled knot of rags and kicked it around as much as he could.

Before long, young Edson found himself with a nickname. It was about

1948 when his friends began calling him Pelé. Most Brazilian soccer players have nicknames. They get them early in life. Some of the nicknames have a meaning. Some don't. Pelé has often said that he doesn't know how he got the name or where it came from or what it means. But it was to stay with him from that time on.

There were other nicknames, too. In Brazil, he is known as Perola Negra (Black Pearl); in France as La Tulipe Noire (The Black Tulip); in Chile as El Peligro (The Dangerous One); and Italy as Il Re (The King). But to most, he is simply Pelé. And that tells the whole story.

Young Pelé was starting school around the time his family moved to Bauru, but he never liked it. He was always thinking about soccer; his grades weren't good. Because schools are not the same in Brazil as they are in the United States, Pelé could decide to leave. So when he was in the fourth grade, he did leave. Now he would just play soccer.

"Soccer was the only career I ever thought of," Pelé said in later years. "I went to work as a cobbler's apprentice for a while when I was young, but I never wanted to stick to it. I wanted to follow my father. I thought he was the greatest soccer player who ever lived. He just never got a chance to prove it."

Like many poor American boys who play baseball and football with very little equipment, Pelé played his first soccer without shoes. In fact, his whole team went barefoot and was called Sete de Setembro. Pelé was eight years old when he first started with this team, and he stayed with them for about five years.

When Pelé was just 11, a man named Valdemar de Brito saw him play for the first time. De Brito was a former

Venezuelan goalie Fazano looks helplessly from the ground as Pelé scores the sixth goal of the game for his Brazilian team.

star of the 1934 Brazil World Cup team. He coached the regular Bauru team, which Pelé's father played for. Coach de Brito quickly saw how good Pelé could be. The youngster was playing in a pickup game against older players. He was by far the best on the field. Right then and there de Brito decided to help young Pelé all he could.

In 1953, the coach formed a junior team in Bauru called Baquinho. It was the first team Pelé played for that had real uniforms. With Pelé as the star, Baquinho won the junior championship three times in a row.

De Brito could see that Pelé was a special king of players. The boy was so much better than all the others on the team. Though he wasn't very big, he already had all the skills needed to be a superstar. He could kick and pass very well with either foot. He had great ball control and could dribble around two or three opposing players. He was very fast and could jump higher than anyone when going for the ball. He knew how to score goals. And, on top of all this, he had the desire to get better and better.

When Pelé was just 14, de Brito decided to take him to several area teams to see if they wanted to sign him. But most teams still felt he was too young and said no. That didn't stop de Brito, who kept telling people everywhere the same thing:

"This boy is going to be the greatest player in the world!"

And de Brito was determined to prove his point. Finally, he took the boy to the coastal city of Santos. Once again, he showed professionals what this 15 year old could do with a soccer ball. This time things were much better. Santos signed Pelé to a contract. They gave him a place to live, his meals, and a small amount of money. He

After converting a penalty, Pelé runs cheerfully to pick up the ball inside the nets.

began his pro career on their junior team.

It wasn't a good beginning. Pelé's first game with the Santos juniors was on June 8, 1956. It was a championship game and Pelé had a chance to tie it near the end with a penalty kick. That's a free kick with only the kicker and the goalkeeper. Good players make this much of the time. But this time Pelé missed and the game was lost.

That didn't bother Pelé for long. He was sorry he missed, but he knew that these things happen to the best of them. After that, his play improved and on September 7, 1956, he played his first game for the regular Santos team.

This time it was a happy occasion. For Pelé was ready. He was just a substitute in the second half, and most of the opposing players felt they'd have no trouble with a 15-year-old- boy. But

Pelé was no ordinary 15 year old. He handled the ball like a veteran. Many times he dribbled around two or three players. He took bulletlike shots at the goal, and made picture-perfect passes to his teammates. Late in the game one of his shots made it through! It was the first of his many, many goals.

There were only a few games left in the 1956 season, but the next year, 1957, Pelé quickly became a regular player. And soon he was a star. He was scoring many goals and people were beginning to watch this flashy 16-year-old striker. That summer Pelé was picked for a Brazilian all-star team that played against a Portuguese team. Pelé scored three goals in that game as Brazil won.

In July of 1957, Pelé played for the Brazil National Team for the first time. The team lost to Argentina, 2–1, but Pelé scored the only goal for

Brazil. Three days later they played again. This time Brazil won 2–0 as Pelé scored again. Scoring was getting to be a habit.

Pelé started another tradition in 1957. After scoring a brilliant goal against Juventus, he suddenly started punching the air with his fist in triumph. It's something he began doing whenever he scored. That meant he was to punch the air more than 1,000 different times.

A year later Pelé had his greatest thrill up to that time. He was picked to represent Brazil on the World Cup team that would be playing in Sweden. He was just a 17 year old and would be playing against the very best soccer players in the entire world for the biggest prize in all soccer.

But once the team arrived in Sweden, Pelé was almost knocked out by an injury. He had a swollen knee and

A jubilant Pelé holds onto the ball with which he
scored his 1,000th goal.

missed the first two games. He got back just in time for the quarter final game against Wales.

It was a hard-fought game. Neither team could manage a score. Then, late in the game, Pelé rocketed one toward the net. The goalkeeper was ready to stop it, when it hit the leg of another Wales player and went in. In some respects it was just plain lucky. But it gave Brazil a 1–0 victory and is a goal Pelé calls the most important of his career.

Next came the semifinal against France. This time Pelé was really on his game. He found the net three times, as Brazil won easily. Now they were in the final against the home team, Sweden. Once again young Pelé was the best player on the field. He scored two goals and set up another as Brazil won the World Cup, 5–2. Pelé never forgot that moment, as he said years later:

"I've played in many worldwide games since then, but if I had to pick one great thrill, it would be the 1958 World Cup. I still shiver when I recall the way the people stood and applauded me after we won the championship game."

It was an unbelievable thing to happen to a 17 year old. Pelé had reached the top of the soccer world in just two years. What could happen next?

Pelé scored 87 goals during the 1958 season. The next year a player called Coutinho came to the Santos team. He was also a striker and played alongside Pelé on the attacking line. Pelé and Coutinho became one of the best striker combinations in history. Their first year together, 1959, Pelé scored a fantastic 127 goals. The two men were

Pelé sails through the air as he kicks the ball back
over his head.

outstanding, as Pelé went on into the 1960s to become the world's greatest soccer player.

Brazil won the Cup again in 1962, though Pelé missed the final games with a pulled muscle. That's how good the rest of the team was by then. In the upcoming years, they got even better, as Pelé himself continued to improve.

He was so important to Brazil they declared him a National Treasure. That way he couldn't be sold to another team. He was also earning more money than anyone else in the sport. By the mid 1960s Pelé was the richest athlete in the entire world. That included all the basketball, football, and baseball superstars in the United States. Pelé's earnings were approaching some two million dollars a year.

The next important year for Pelé was 1966. It was a year of both good and bad things. By the time Brazil went into World Cup play, Pelé was already known as the King of Soccer. Many players on other teams wanted to stop him. But they weren't as good as Pelé. The only way they could stop him was to play dirty soccer.

In the first game against Bulgaria, Pelé scored on a long, curving free kick from the corner. Later in that game, he was badly fouled by two Bulgarian players who stepped on his leg. He limped to the sidelines and missed the second game against Hungary. He returned to play against Benfica of Portugal. But he was again injured on a foul and had to sit out the rest of the games. Brazil didn't win the Cup that year, and Pelé was very angry because his opponents had played dirty.

"If it is going to be like this," he said, "I will never play in a World Cup game again."

Something else happened during that 1966 World Cup series. A player from the Benfica team named Eusebio had a brilliant series. He scored nine goals in six Cup games. In one game against North Korea, he had four goals. People began calling Eusebio the new Pelé, the new King of Soccer. But Eusebio didn't want that title.

"I feel that calling me the new Pelé was very unfair both for Pelé and me," said Eusebio. "To me, Pelé is the greatest soccer player of all time. I only hope that one day I can be the second best ever."

Eusebio knew what he was talking about. Later that same year a special match was set up between Pelé's Santos team and Eusebio's Benfica club. It was held in New York before some 30,000 fans.

This time it was Pelé's day. He scored one goal and set up three others with sharp passes. Santos won, 4–0. Late in the game, he streaked back on defense to steal the ball right

Pelé is stopped by a crowd while riding in an open jeep down the Champs Elysees in Paris.

from Eusebio. Then he raced off the other way, saluting Eusebio as he went. That was Pelé's pride talking. He was just reminding everyone that he was still the best, Eusebio agreed:

"I told you not to say bad things about him," Eusebio told the press. "He's still as great as ever, and he'll stay that way until the day he retires."

Off the field there was another milestone for Pelé. In 1966 he was married to a woman named Rosemarie Cholby. People were surprised. Very few knew about her. But that's because Pelé is a very private man. He doesn't want his great public soccer career getting in the way of his personal life. He and Rosemarie were engaged for six years. In that time Pelé never took her out in public, and she never came to a jam-packed stadium to watch him play.

It has been a happy marriage. Pelé and Rosemarie have two children—a girl, Kelly Christina, born in 1967, and

Pelé and the former Rosemarie Cholby on their wedding day.

a boy, Edson Cholby do Nascimento, born in 1970. The boy had a nickname by the time he was six, Edinho. Perhaps someday fans will chant that name as they do the name of his famous father.

There were many chants of Pelé's name during the next years. Pelé and his Santos team won the San Paulo State Championship for three straight years. Then on November 11, 1969, Pelé made history by scoring his 1,000th goal. The people in Brazil began begging the 29-year-old Pelé to forget his past feelings and play in another World Cup.

It is fortunate for the soccer world that he did, for Pelé was brilliant throughout the entire series. In the opening round, he scored six times in six games. Besides the scoring, he was all over the field. He got back on defense, helped his teammates, and set them up for other scoring chances.

Brazil advanced to the final round of the 1970 World Cup tournament and in these games he was just as good, scoring four more times. He also got the first goal in the final game against Italy to start Brazil on the way to a 4–1 victory. It was the third World Cup for Brazil since Pelé had joined the national team. Once again, he was hailed as the greatest soccer player in the world. It seemed as if Pelé had no more worlds to conquer.

By 1971, there were signs that Pelé was getting tired of it all. First, he announced his last appearance with the Brazilian National Team. When he appeared with them at Paris, it was a gala sight. There were some 100,000 fans, all shouting his name. And, as usual, he played brilliantly.

Then in July, he played at Maracana Stadium in Rio de Janeiro. It was his final game for the National Team in Brazil. Some 120,000 fans kept screaming his name throughout the game. When it was over, he took his famous number 10 jersey in his hand and jogged around the field, as everyone cried:

STAY . . . STAY . . . STAY . . . STAY

But Pelé meant what he said. He continued to play for Santos until September of 1974 because there was another World Cup that year. But he kept his word and didn't play for the National Team. Then on September 22, he scored his last goal for Santos. And on October 2, 1974, he played his final game for his longtime team. When he left the field, the fans kept applauding and screaming for their idol. There were tears running down Pelé's face. But it looked as if there were no turning back. After 18 years, the one and only Pelé had retired.

Pelé's farewell to his Brazilian fans.

CHAPTER 3

Pelé's retirement was not really to last very long. Things were happening in the United States that would soon shake up the entire soccer world. Since 1967, people in the United States had been trying to get soccer to become a bigger sport.

In fact, two new leagues formed in this country in 1967. One was the United States Association and the other the National Professional Soccer League. The first brought 12 teams from other countries to play in the United States. The second formed 10

In Tokyo's National Stadium, Pelé teaches the techniques of soccer to a young Japanese player.

new teams with players from the United States and other countries. So in one year there were 22 professional soccer teams across America. It was too much at one time. The two leagues merged in 1968 and formed the North American Soccer League with 17 teams. But the crowds were very small, and at the end of the year most of the teams went out of business.

It looked bad at the beginning of 1969. If the league folded, pro soccer might be dead in the United States for another 20 years. So NASL officials didn't want to quit. They opened the 1969 season with just five teams—Atlanta, Baltimore, Dallas, Kansas City, and St. Louis. Somehow, those five stayed alive.

New leagues always have teams coming and going their first few years. In 1970, there were six teams; Washington and Rochester joining,

Baltimore dropping out. Then in 1971, the NASL grew to eight teams, with Kansas City dropping out and Montreal, New York, and Toronto joining.

The New York team was called the Cosmos. And like most new leagues, a strong New York team was very important for the league's success. It didn't take long for the Vice-President and General Manager of the Cosmos, Clive Toye, to think up a great idea: What if Pelé were to come to New York and play for the Cosmos?

Toye wasted no time. Just a month after the Cosmos started, he flew to Kingston, Jamaica. There he met with Pelé, who was still playing with the Santos team.

"I just wanted to tell him about soccer in the United States and how we hoped it would grow," said Toye. "At the same time I wanted him to re-

Pelé waves to the crowd in Philadelphia after the Cosmos announced his signing.

member the Cosmos. I told him we'd be back to see him as soon as he decided to leave Santos."

That began a four and one-half year effort by the Cosmos to sign Pelé and bring him to New York. During that time the North American Soccer League continued to grow. The league went into California for the first time, with teams in Los Angeles, San Francisco, and Seattle. It also expanded into Canada, with a team in Vancouver, British Columbia. It was now a coast-to-coast league.

By 1973 there were 9 teams and the next year 15. There were more people coming to the games than ever before—an average of 7,825 a game in 1974. And four of the league's teams averaged more than 10,000 fans a game.

That was the same year Pelé refused to play in the World Cup and later retired from Santos. And that was also the year Clive Toye began to really try to get Pelé to play for the Cosmos. In July of 1974, he met with Pelé and Pelé's advisor, Professor Julio Mazzei. Toye made the first real offer for Pelé to play with the Cosmos.

When the NASL opened the 1975 season with 20 teams, most people agreed Pelé was the one man who could put the league over the top. For the first time in history, there was a chance for soccer to become a major sport in the United States.

By early 1975 Pelé seemed interested in playing with the Cosmos. In April he said no to one offer. But by the end of May, he had changed his mind. Then, in early June, the word came that Pelé was coming to New York.

Reporters began to flock around Pelé whenever they could. They all asked the same questions: Was he coming out of retirement? And why would he choose the Cosmos instead of returning to Santos? Though he spoke little English, Pelé was always very patient with North American reporters. He always had a friend with him who could tell him the questions and then tell the reporters Pelé's answers. Such a person is called an interpreter.

There was a special reason Pelé was thinking of coming out of retirement. Many people thought it would be for the money. They said the Cosmos would pay Pelé millions of dollars. But Pelé already had a great deal of money from the years before. If he played again, it would be for just one reason—his love for the game of soccer.

"If an offer had come to me from West Germany, Spain, Italy, or even Brazil, I would have said no," Pelé

President Ford watches as Pelé bounces a ball off his head. Pelé later gave the ball to the President.

explained, carefully. "That would be a different principle. But to return to playing in the United States is a different thing.

"I love soccer. I've been playing it for 20 years around the world. So why should I not come to the United States and try to help the game? New York is a great place for sports. I really feel if I come here, I could give something to United States soccer."

Then someone asked Pelé how the Brazilian people would feel. After all, he was a national hero in that country. Many people felt he should play for them and no one else.

"Naturally, the Brazilian people would prefer that I play in Brazil," said Pelé. "But I think they would be proud of me if Brazil got some recognition by my playing soccer here."

On June 10, 1975, Pelé signed a three-year contract to play with the

Cosmos. It was a huge contract. The full terms were never announced. But the entire package was said to be worth between 4.5 and 7 million dollars. That was not only for games, but also for promotional work for Warner Communications, the company that represented him.

CHAPTER 4

The season had already started when Pelé joined the Cosmos in June. Everyone wanted to know how soon he could get in shape. After all, the King of Soccer was 34 years old. That is an age when most professional athletes begin to slip past their primes. Pelé had been away from the game for nearly a year. That can sometimes make an athlete's skills disappear even faster. But Pelé explained that he had not been away from the game completely. He had played some exhibition games and wasn't worried.

"I'm in fine shape," he said. "I never really stopped training. In fact, I just got finished playing five games over in Europe."

That wasn't all. People who knew Pelé said he was truly an amazing athlete. Not a big man, he stands barely five feet, eight inches tall. He has often called his athletic ability one of "God's divine gifts." But medical men said there was more to it than that.

One doctor noted that Pelé's heart beats 56 to 58 times a minute. The average athlete's heart beats 90 to 95 times a minute. That means he has exceptional stamina and can repeat a great effort within 45 to 60 seconds. Tests on his eyes showed that his peripheral vision, which is the ability to see things on the side, is 30 percent better than the average athlete.

He also has very strong feet and heel bones, enabling him to run better and absorb more impact on jumps and high kicks. At 34, Pelé could still run the 100 meters in 11 seconds, and jump 6 feet in the air. Soccer experts say he can jump sooner than other players when going for the ball. Like some great basketball players, Pelé seems to hover in the air a split second longer than others.

Julio Mazzei, Pelé's longtime friend, said of Pelé's athletic ability:

"If properly trained, Pelé could still be one of the world's 10 best in the decathlon. And he can play both volleyball and basketball magnificently."

And one doctor, who once gave Pelé a whole series of physical tests, remarked:

"Whatever this man might have decided to do in any physical or mental endeavor, he would have been a genius."

Cosmos teammate John Kerr and Pelé congratulate each other after Pelé made an assist on a goal during an exhibition game against the Dallas Tornado at New York's Downing Stadium on Randalls Island.

The King of Soccer dribbling.

Pelé himself knows the things he can do. But he still explains it as "God's divine gifts."

"I feel the divine gift to make something out of nothing," he said. "You need balance and speed of mind and strength. But there is something else that God has given me. It's an extra instinct I have for the game. Sometimes I can take the ball and no one can foresee any danger. And then, two or three seconds later, there is a goal. This doesn't make me proud, it makes me humble because it is a talent that God gave me."

One thing is for sure. Pelé's skills will allow him to score many goals for a long time. And as soon as he signed with the Cosmos, more fans than ever began making plans to see him play. This is just what the North American Soccer League hoped for.

Pelé scissor-kicks.

CHAPTER 5

Pelé's new teammates on the Cosmos soon found out what it was like to play with the King of Soccer. Goalkeeper Sam Nusum remembers the first practice session. Pelé had the ball at halfcourt during an indoor practice. He dribbled past two defenders and was facing Nusum head on. Instead of shooting, he just smiled and passed the ball back to a teammate.

"I think if he shot the ball, he might have torn my head off," Nusum said. "I've seen how hard he can kick. You know, until today, I've only seen him on film. But after today, you can see he has every move in the book."

Another new teammate, Alfredo Lamas, was thought to be the Cosmos best dribbler. But every time he tried to dribble past Pelé, the ball wound up going the other way. Though Pelé wasn't yet in top shape, everyone could see he was still great.

The first game he played was a special exhibition against the Dallas Tornado. The Tornado had an American-born star, Kyle Rote, Jr. The game was played in late June before some 21,278 fans at Downing Stadium in New York.

Many players on the Cosmos spoke different languages because they came from other countries. Yet it was obvious that Pelé was directing them on the field, or trying to. Sometimes he made brilliant moves past the Tornado defenders. But his clever and sharp passes often caught his own teammates unaware. At halftime, Dallas held a 2–0 lead.

Then in the second half, Pelé started to take charge. First he made a perfect pass to teammate Mordechai Shpigler, an Israeli, who booted the ball past the Dallas goalkeeper to make it a 2–1 game.

Nine minutes later, Shpigler lofted a high pass near the goal. Pelé leaped higher than the Dallas player and snapped his head. The ball shot into the net and the game was tied. Pelé leaped high again, punching the air as he always does on a goal. And the large crowd began chanting:

PELÉ . . . PELÉ . . . PELÉ . . . PELÉ

After the game, Pelé had to answer newsmen's questions again. Wherever he goes, the reporters flock around. But Pelé always answers all the questions with a smile on his face. And one

Pelé fakes a defender.

thing he never does is criticize team-mates as individuals.

"We have a lot of different styles," he said of that game. "We must learn to help each other and play as a team."

Pelé was impressed with Dallas, especially young Kyle Rote, Jr.

"Kyle Rote has a great deal of skill, considering he's an American who has been playing the game only about six or seven years."

He said that because soccer players the world over play the game from childhood. And one of Pelé goals was to get American youngsters to play that way, too.

Pelé's playing brought more and more people out to the soccer field that season. The last week in June, the Cosmos traveled to Boston to play the Minutemen who had signed an old rival of Pelé's—the great Eusebio. There was a huge crowd at the stadium. They were lined up all around the field, screaming for the start of the game.

It was a hard-fought game and the excitement was high. Suddenly, without warning, hundreds of fans began swarming on the field. Most of them ran to Pelé, pressing in closer and closer. They did not really mean to harm him, but in the crush of people he was knocked to the ground. For safety's sake, Pelé was carried off the field on a stretcher. He had a slightly bruised ankle and knee. But he was all right.

Perhaps Pelé understood what happened better than most. Soccer fans in other parts of the world have always been very excitable. But the Cosmos management was upset. They wanted more protection.

"This must not happen again," said a Cosmos spokesman. "We must have more security. The people were too close to the sideline. To play a game

Getting set to head a pass.

under those conditions was not fair to Pelé, to Eusebio, or the other players."

After that, the league controlled the crowds. There had been 22,000 fans in that 15,000-seat stadium in Boston. That wouldn't happen again. Now Pelé could concentrate on playing soccer. And that's what he wanted to do in the first place.

In a 9–2 Cosmos win against Washington, a player named Roy Willner couldn't believe Pelé's ability.

"I've never seen a guy jump so high without running," Willner said. "He's got the best spring in his legs I've ever seen. When I learned I'd be guarding him, I looked at some films trying to find a weakness. Believe me, it's useless. There's no way to stop the guy without knocking him out, and I'm not that type of player.

"Twice I thought I had him stopped. Both times he made me look like a fool. Once he went right around me and the other time he feinted in one direction, went the other way, and I found myself bumping into one of my teammates."

Against the Rochester Lancers, Pelé scored the first goal in a 3–0 Cosmos win. Lancer goalie Ardo Perri was now a Pelé believer.

"I still don't know where he came from," said Perri. "You can't take yours eyes off him for a second. I made a couple of early saves on him, but I guess that was luck. I've played against top forwards in my life, but believe me, there is only one Pelé."

In a late July game against Toronto, Pelé was hurt. That was the thing the whole league feared most. And it happened because of Pelé's great skills.

It was early in the second half and Pelé made one of his moves, dribbling past one defender and then around another. When he started to move past a third, the man kicked at the ball. But Pelé was so quick the kick missed the ball and caught Pelé in the thigh. It was a bad bruise. It caused him to miss several games. But when he came back he was better than ever.

Later, when the Cosmos played Boston again, Pelé was brilliant. He was all over the field. He played well on both offense and defense. Cosmos Coach Gorden Bradley couldn't say enough about his star striker.

"He kept bouncing up from hard tackles and fouls, and he was often sprinting 40 yards to take the ball away from a Boston attacker. The man is just incredible."

In another game against Vancouver, Lee Wilson of the Whitecaps also tried to stop Pelé.

"I was faked out many, many times. When I backed off him, expecting him to try to dribble, he would put a loft pass right over my head onto the feet of one of his teammates. Then when I'd try to get real close to him, he'd back off the ball to get a running start and take off.

"I've never seen a man read the game so well in my life. He knows where every man on his team is at every time. After the game he came over to me and told me that I played a pretty good game. I'm glad he told me so because I think he made me look like a fool."

That is something else about Pelé. He always has a friendly word for everyone: his teammates, his opponents, and the fans. No matter how famous Pelé may become, he will never change as a man. Carlos Alberto was a teammate of Pelé's on the Brazilian National Team. He remembers how Pelé was then.

Pelé passes ball through the legs of a defender.

"Pelé was always the same to all of us. He never acted like the star or like a hero. If I needed a soda, Pelé would be the first to get it for me."

Roy Willner of Washington feels the same way. "I never asked an athlete for an autograph before in my life," said Willner. "But after playing against Pelé I just had to get his name on the game program. He's not only the greatest soccer player in the world, he's one of the nicest men I ever met."

And after almost every game, Pelé spends time signing autographs for fans. He always has a friendly word for the kids. Ted Howard of the North American Soccer League talked about the kind of man Pelé is off the soccer field:

"He's an individual who is a tre-mendously fascinating person, but he's not the kind who creates problems. He has a tremendous image. In fact, he's one of the most beautiful people I've ever met. The newspaper people love him. They come in thinking that someone with all that money and that career would be arrogant. But when they meet him they realize he's not.

"I remember catching a ride on the Cosmos team bus after a game in Washington. We were supposed to keep the windows closed so the air conditioning could work. But people kept recognizing Pelé, and he kept opening the window, reaching out and shaking hands, and signing auto-graphs. He'll sign autographs until his arm falls off."

But that's Pelé. He himself said many times, "I have always believed that no matter how much fame a man has, he should live a simple life."

Pelé hasn't changed, despite being a worldwide hero. And he is still a great soccer player. Once he was in shape and free of injury, he played brilliant soccer. But the Cosmos could have used some other top players, for even with Pelé, they finished the season with a 10–12 record. (After Pelé joined, they won seven and lost six.)

Because of his injury, Pelé played in just nine regular season games. In those games he scored five goals and had four assists. But that wasn't all. The Cosmos played 14 other games. They were exhibitions. Some of them were against very good teams from other countries. In those 14 games, Pelé had 10 goals and 10 assists. That was more like it.

The NASL counts two points for a goal and one for an assist. So in 23 total games, Pelé had 15 goals and 14 assists, good for 44 points. And don't forget, he didn't join the team until near midseason. So at age 34, he remained a superstar of the game.

Pelé tells Boston Minutemen's Bill Wilkinson to use his head!

CHAPTER 6

Pelé has done much for soccer. For instance, league attendance is better than ever. And it looks like it will keep getting better in the upcoming years. There are also more American youngsters playing soccer than ever before. In addition, other top world players are coming to the NASL to play. The league is trying to get better. They still want the top foreign players. But there are also more Americans coming in. That's a good thing for American fans.

Soccer also helped celebrate the American Bicentennial. There was a

Meeting his new coach, Ken Furphy.

big tournament in the summer of 1976. Pelé played for Team America, with national teams from England, Italy, and Brazil joining the action. There was more soccer than ever in the United States.

Pelé is helping all this to happen. After the 1974 season, Mike Gansell, who coaches the John F. Kennedy High team in New York, told how Pelé is helping his players.

"Up to last year," said Coach Gansell, "we never scored a goal on a head shot. That's one of Pelé's biggest strengths. He can jump over his man and score on a head shot. Our kids saw that. Now the first thing you know we have six goals on head shots."

That's what league officials hope Pelé can do all over. This is the first real chance soccer has had in the United States. It's showing signs of life.

A Brazilian has given all this help to American soccer—a man who started playing for 140 dollars a year as a 15 year old and ended up playing for millions. He's a man who once stopped a civil war in the African country of Biafra. There was a truce called so both sides could come watch him play. He's a man who has played before countless numbers of fans. And whether they've rooted for or against him, they've all admitted the same thing . . .

The man called Pelé is without a doubt the very best—The King of Soccer.

"Every moment is happiness," says Pelé of his stay in the United States, during a quiet moment in his New York office.